Collins

Knowledge Lighthouse 2

A skill-based course on General Knowledge

Seema Chari
Kunal Savarkar

Student + Teacher						Teacher-only			
a	animations	**ia**	activities	**g**	games	**lp**	lesson plans	**tn**	teacher's notes
ilt	instructor-led tutorials	**w**	worksheets	**v**	videos	**w**	worksheets	**ak**	answer keys
		🔊	audio						

Preface

There is no single route to knowledge and its sources are as diverse as the paths we adopt to gather and retain it, right from our family, school and friends to the Internet and books. General Knowledge is like common sense, but in times of multimedia, while it is easily available and accessible, it is not always easy to distinguish between real and fake, relevant and redundant, and interesting and inconsequential. We live in the digital age, which requires constant flexibility and adaptability.

Knowledge Lighthouse is a series meant for the Gen Z, or learners born in the new millennium. Their professional requirements are drastically different from those of earlier generations and require 'upskilling' throughout their lives. The series covers the general knowledge quotient of a spectrum of curricular as well as extra-curricular domains for learners of grades 1 to 8, with special emphasis on 21st century skills. They are divided into three segments—learning skills, literacy skills and life skills. Through this series, we are certain that all learners can attain knowledge as the tasks are 'workoutable' and grade-appropriate.

General Knowledge provides context to school curriculum. *Knowledge Lighthouse* books are a repository of varied tasks divided in eight themes and skill pages. Our country is often presented in a complicated or insufficient way in GK books. This series showcases India content through colourful, simple and exciting tasks. Within the vast and varied India chapters are brand-new features such as state-focus, city-focus and visit-a-monument.

Science, technology, engineering and mathematics (STEM), the disciplines of the future that add a sprinkle of trivia to otherwise serious subjects have been covered extensively in grades 6-8.

The protection of our planet and sustainable development are critical issues that all of us need to think about and be aware of. Save the Planet theme aims to sensitise learners towards sustainable development throughout the series.

In the Skills pages, life skills has tasks on safety and self-awareness. Connecting the dots is the foundation of knowledge and the series has chapters based on Higher Order Thinking Skills (HOTS) and critical thinking to train young minds to see patterns, learn to eliminate or choose details and observe better.

Become a Champion Quizzer

Knowledge Lighthouse encourages all learners to be curious and explore the world around them. Those who observe and absorb all the time, learn from everyone and everything; they are the ones who become quizzers! Here are six rules that will help you become a champion quizzer.

1. Be curious—look around you, see everything, read everything.
2. Listen to others.
3. Seek out new experiences.
4. Learn to link events and people.
5. Do your own research and learn to spot fake news.
6. Remember, no matter how much you know, there is much more that you have yet to learn.

Now, go for it! We are sure that this series will expose a whole new generation of learners to the fun universe of general knowledge, and enhance their love for learning and discovery.

~ Kunal Savarkar and Seema Chari

In this series ...

Knowledge Lighthouse tasks are thematic and linear with visual, verbal, and strategic inputs to help students solve them and acquire knowledge through a wide range of subjects and themes.

World Around Us tasks take the learners on an exciting journey across the world.

Our Natural World section uncovers the magical realm of plants, animals and birds.

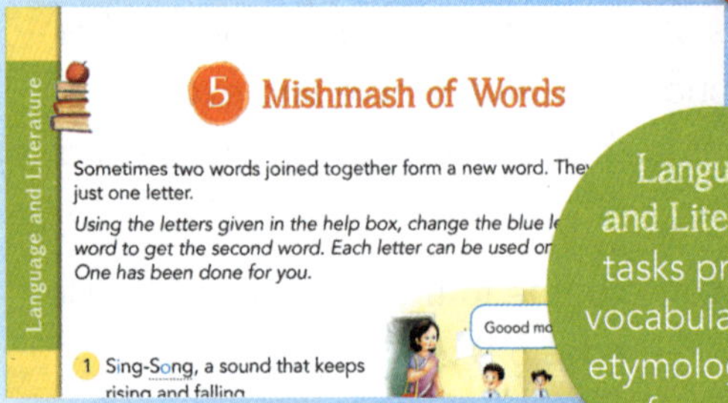

Language and Literature tasks present vocabulary and etymology in a fun way.

India tasks are created to evoke a sense of wonder and pride in our nation.

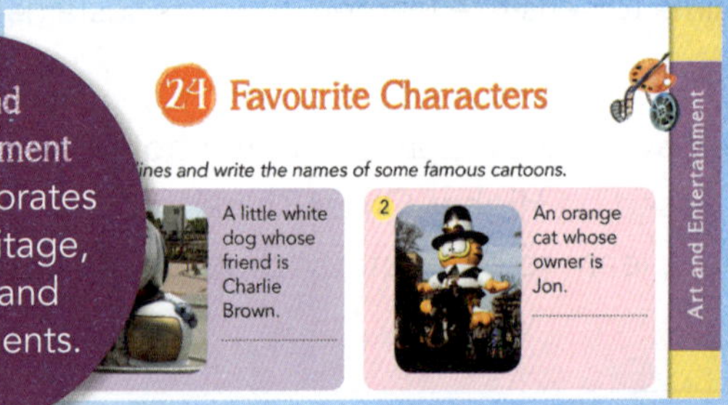

Art and Entertainment tasks celebrates world heritage, awards and achievements.

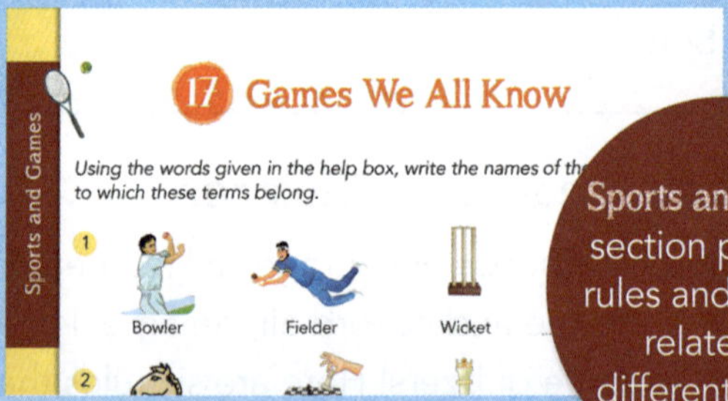

Sports and Games section provides rules and records related to different sports.

Save the Planet sensitises learners towards sustainable development of the planet.

Whiz Quiz are fun activities that encourage self-learning.

Whiz Fact is a spin-off fact about each topic or theme.

21st Century Skills

21st century skills are necessary to succeed in the Age of Information. These skills are divided into three main sets, namely, learning skills, literacy skills and life skills.

Learning Skills
Critical Thinking and HOTS
Creativity
Collaboration
Communication

39 Filling Up

Look at these containers. What would you fill them with? Draw a line to join the container to the correct answers.

1 Glass
2 Can
3 Cup
4 Spoon
5 Bucket
c Water

Learning Skills
CRITICAL THINKING

Literacy Skills
Technology
Information
Media

20 Lucky Seven

...te these lists all of which have seven words. The first letter ...word has been given.

Days of the Week
S ...... T ......
M ...... F ......
T ...... S ......
W ......

Colours of the Rainbow
V ...... Y ......
I ...... O ......
B ...... R ......
G ......

Disney's Seven Dwarfs
D ...... S ......
G ...... B ......
H ...... S ......
D ......

Musical Notes

4

Literacy Skills
INFORMATION

Life Skills
Problem-solving
Self-awareness
Safety
Social Skills

3 The Right Words

Can you find the right words to say in each of these situations? Fill in the blanks with the right words given in the help box.

1 You sneeze
2 Your friend wins a prize
3
4

Life Skills
SOCIAL SKILLS

Detailed Contents

Sports and Games

- Games We All Know
- Sports Places

Save the Planet

- Clean and Green

Learning Skills

- Shapes of Things
- Dress Up
- In the Park
- Filling Up
- Monster Shadows

Literacy Skills

- Lucky Seven
- Animal and Bird Logos
- Computer World

Life Skills

- The Right Words
- Play Safe
- Spot the Differences
- First Aid Kit

Contents

1 Words About Birds

We can describe a person or an object by comparing it with another thing. Here are some birds that are used to describe a person or a thing.

Complete the phrases with the names of the birds given in the help box. One has been done for you.

1 

As happy as a lark

2 

As wise as an ....

3 

As black as a ....

4 

As graceful as a ....

5 

As talkative as a ....

6 

As proud as a ....

crow peacock parrot swan owl

Whiz Fact

The first birds were not soft and feathery. They had leathery wings and claws, and were actually dinosaurs!

2 Our Five Senses

We have five senses. We use them to see, hear, smell, taste, touch or feel.

Look at these pictures and fill in the blanks using the words given in the help box.

1 

I ....

2 

I ....

3 

I ....

4 

I ....

see hear smell taste touch feel

5

I..

6

I..

7

I..

8

I..

9

I..

Whiz Fact

The parts of the body such as eyes, ears, skin and nose are called sense organs. They enable us to be aware of things around us.

3 The Right Words

Can you find the right words to say in each of these situations? Fill in the blanks with the right words given in the help box.

1

You sneeze

....

2

Your friend wins a prize

....

3

The teacher says you are going for a picnic

....

4

Your friend meets you in the park

....

5

Your friend gives you a gift ....

6

You step on your friend's toe by mistake ....

7

Your friend is going to bed ....

8

Your friend wants to borrow your book ....

yay I am sorry please goodnight
congratulations excuse me hello thank you

Whiz Fact

The right way to behave in public is called etiquette. The word etiquette was first used in France for the correct way to behave in a king's court.

4 Daily Activities

Be a logic detective. Here are some activities Tina does from morning till the time she comes home from school. However, they are jumbled up.

Look at the pictures and put them in the correct order by writing letters.

1

Tina reaches home. ☐

2

Tina catches school bus. ☐

3

Tina reaches school. ☐

4

Tina gets dressed for school. ☐

5

Tina brushes her teeth. ☐

6

Tina eats breakfast. ☐

7

Tina eats a sandwich. ☐

8

Tina leaves from school. ☐

9

Tina wakes up. ☐

10

Tina eats lunch at home. ☐

Whiz Quiz

Write three activities you do when you return from school in the correct order.

1 ....

2 ....

3 ....

5 Mishmash of Words

Sometimes two words joined together form a new word. They differ by just one letter.

Using the letters given in the help box, change the blue letter in each word to get the second word. Each letter can be used only once. One has been done for you.

1 Sing-Song, a sound that keeps rising and falling.

2 Ding- .... , goes the bell.

3 Knick- .... , a little thing used for decoration.

4 Tip- .... , feeling great.

5 Pitter- .... , fall the raindrops.

6 Tick- .... , goes the clock.

7 Dilly- .... , wasting time.

8 Ping- .... , we play table tennis.

9 Humpty- .... sat on a wall.

10 Zig- .... , moving left, then right, then left, then right.

a d o a o a o o a

Whiz Fact

An old word that means 'nonsense' is pish-tosh.

6 Shapes of Things

Join the dots to draw the shapes of these objects and write the names of the shapes using the words given in the help box.

1

....

2

....

3

....

4

....

5

....

6

....

Whiz Quiz

A triangle has three sides and three corners. How many sides and corners does a rectangle have?

7

8

9

10

11

12

13

14

circle square rectangle triangle oval

Whiz Fact

Pebbles on river banks are almost always oval. They have no sharp edges because the flowing water makes them smooth.

7 Baby Animals

Animals and their babies have different names. Match the babies to their parents.

1  Calf

2  Puppy

3  Kitten

4  Lamb

5  Foal

a  Sheep

b  Horse

c  Dog

d  Cat

e  Cow

Whiz Fact

Many baby names are made by adding -let or -ling at the end of the names of parents. So, a baby eagle is called an eaglet. A baby goose is called a gosling and a baby duck is called a duckling.

8 Clean and Green

Tick (✓) the activities that are good for the environment and cross (✗) the ones that are bad.

1

Burning leaves

2

Planting trees

3

Washing clothes in rivers

4

Leaving dustbins uncovered

5

Cycling to work

6

Cutting trees

Whiz Fact

When you eat outdoors or while travelling, always carry a sheet of newspaper. You can wrap the leftovers in it and throw it in a dustbin.

9 Jobs People Do

People do different jobs and make beautiful things. Write the names of these people using the words given in the help box.

1

A .... makes our gardens beautiful.

2

A .... makes chairs and tables.

3

A .... makes beautiful paintings.

4

A .... sews clothes.

Whiz Fact Writing poems, songs, jokes or giving ideas are creative jobs. We cannot touch, taste or smell these things but we can read, hear or feel them.

5

A .... makes pots, vases and bowls.

6

A .... mends shoes.

7

A .... makes necklaces, rings and earrings

8

A .... makes cakes.

cobbler	tailor	carpenter	gardener
painter	potter	jeweller	baker

Whiz Quiz

Find out what jobs do the following people do:

1. Mason ....
2. Farmer ....

10 Big Animals

Write the names of some big animals in the crossword with the help of the clues.

Across

2 An animal with a hump that lives in deserts.

4 A big fish with very sharp teeth.

6 A big and heavy animal that lives near water and has legs that look like fins.

7 A furry, white animal that lives in very cold regions and eats seals and fish.

8 A large animal that hops around and carries its babies in a pocket.

10 A black, hairy animal that lives in forests and has hands like human beings.

Down

1 A big grey animal with a horn on its head.

3 A big grey animal with a long trunk and two long teeth called tusks.

5 An animal with huge mouth and short legs. It spends a lot of time in water.

9 The tallest animal in the world with a very long neck.

Whiz Fact

Blue whale is the largest animal on the Earth. Its tongue is as heavy as an elephant!

Whiz Quiz

1 .... is the fastest animal on land.

2 .... is the slowest animal on land.

11 Dress Up

Four best friends are packing for vacations but their clothes are mixed up.

Using colours as clues, match the clothes and things to the children by writing numbers. Each child should have four things to pack. One has been done for you.

1 
Sweater

2 
Stockings

3 
T-shirt

4 
Flip flops

5 
Hat

6 
Sneakers

7 
Cap

8 
Purse

a 

b 

Whiz Fact

If a drawer is full of red socks and green socks and you want a matching pair, how many socks should you take out without looking? You will need only three. Try it out.

9

Boots

10

Blouse

11

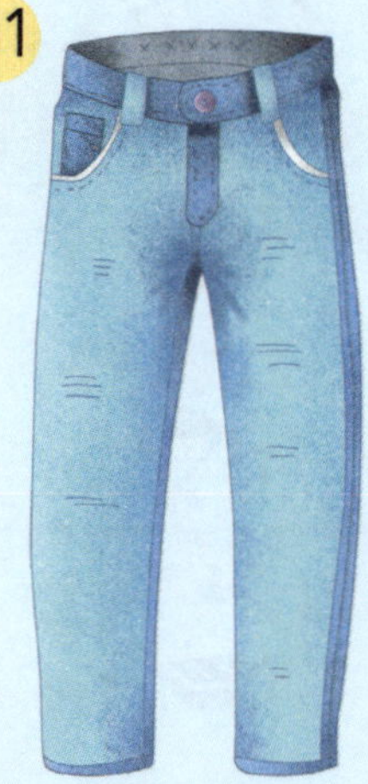

Jeans

12

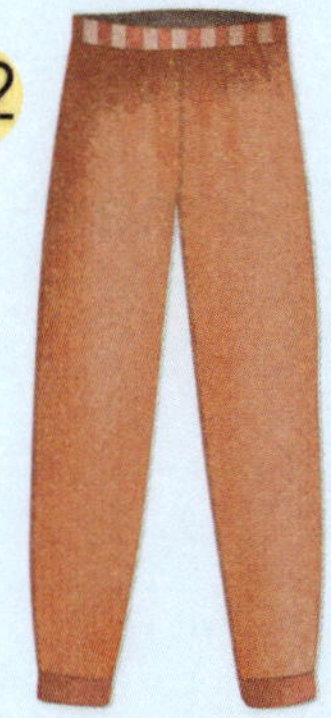

Woollen trousers

13

Backpack

14

Shoes

15

Dress

16

Skirt

c

d

12 Things Used at Work

Match these people with the things they use at work.

1 Farmer  | a 

2 Cobbler  | b 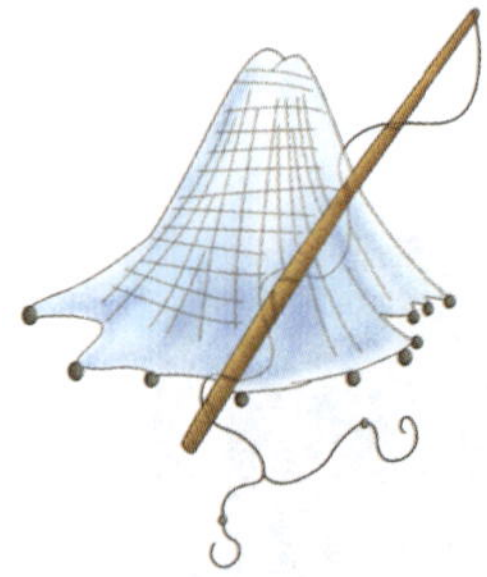

3 Baker  | c 

4 Tailor  | d 

5 Fisherman  | e 

6 Gardener

f

7 Flight attendant

g

8 Cartoonist

h

9 Tattooist

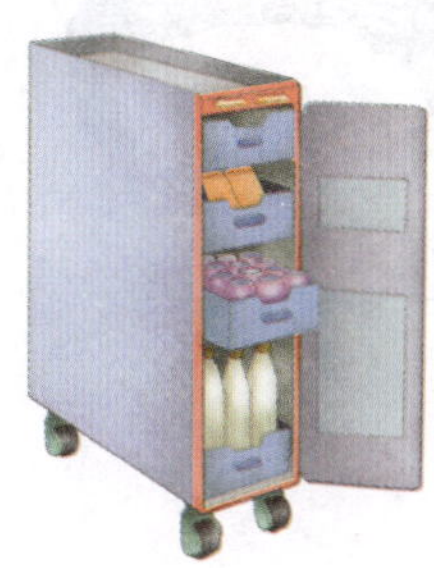

i

10 Disc jockey

j

Whiz Fact

A quizmaster needs no tools, only a brain, lots of knowledge and a list of fun questions.

13 Farm to Fork

Let us see how things we eat are made. Write 1, 2 or 3 to put the pictures in correct sequence. One has been done for you.

1

Jam 3

Fruit 2

Plant 1

2

Omelette ☐

Hen ☐

Egg ☐

3

Dried leaves ☐

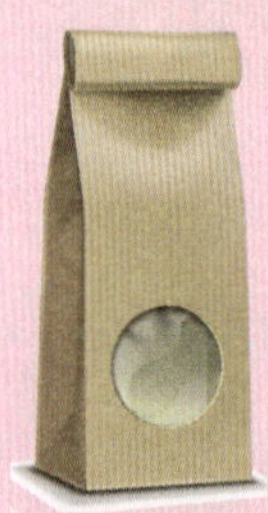
Tea packet ☐

Tea leaves ☐

4

Milk ☐

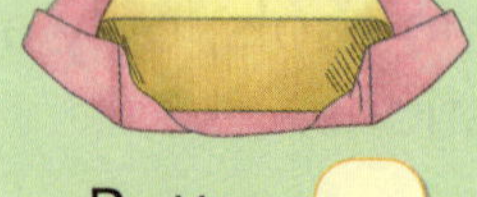
Butter ☐

Cow ☐

5

Honeybee ☐

Honey ☐

Beehive ☐

6

Coconut chutney ☐

Coconut tree ☐

Coconut ☐

7

Lemons ☐

Juice ☐

Lemon plant ☐

8

Cocoa beans ☐

Chocolate ☐

Cocoa tree ☐

Whiz Fact

Honey never spoils if stored in a properly closed jar or a container. It can stay good for many years!

14 Games of India

Look at the pictures and write the names of some famous games of India using the words given in the help box.

1 ....

2 ....

3 ....

4 ....

hide-and-seek   gilli danda   skipping   seven stones
kho kho   marbles   kite flying   hopscotch

5 ....

6 ....

7 ....

8 ....

Whiz Fact

Kabaddi is one of the oldest sports in the world. It was first played in India.

15 Oh! Look at the Moon!

Some words are missing from this lovely poem about the moon. Complete the poem with the help of the pictures and the words given in the help box.

Oh! look at the moon,
She is shining up there;
Oh! Mother, she looks
Like a 1 .... in the air.

Last week she was smaller,
And shaped like a 2 ....
But now she's grown bigger,
And round as an 3 ....

Pretty moon, pretty moon,
How you shine on the 4 .... ,
And make it all bright
On my nursery 5 ....

Whiz Fact

The famous poem 'Twinkle, Twinkle, Little Star' was written by the poet, Jane Taylor.

You shine on my 6 .... ,
And show me their place,
And I love to look up
At your pretty bright 7 ....

And there is the 8 ....
Close by you, and maybe
That small, twinkling star
Is your little 9 ....

– Eliza Lee Cabot Follen

playthings	face	star	lamp	bow
O	door	baby	floor	

Whiz Quiz

Using five words from the help box, write a poem of your own.

16 Animal Homes

Write the names of the homes of our animal-friends using the words given in the help box.

Horse

1

....

2

Dog

....

3

Cow

....

Whiz Quiz

Name two animals who build their homes.

1 ....

2 ....

kennel coop shed pen
stable pond

4

Duck

....

5

Hen

....

6

Sheep

....

Whiz Fact

Animals such as cats and dogs that live in our homes are called pets or domestic animals. Animals that live in forest are called wild animals.

17 Games We All Know

Using the words given in the help box, write the names of the games to which these terms belong.

1

Bowler

Fielder

Wicket

....

2

Knight

Checkmate

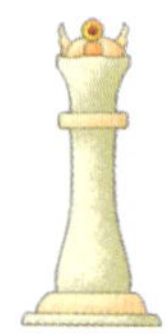
Queen

....

3

Goalpost

Referee

Red card

....

4

Dribble

Lay-up

Basket

....

basketball   football   chess   cricket

Whiz Fact

India does not have an official national game. Cricket and hockey are popular games of India.

18 Special Days

All Indians celebrate or observe these days in honour of their country and its people.

Write the dates on which we celebrate these special days using the help box.

1 

Mahatma Gandhi's' birthday

....

2 

Jawaharlal Nehru's birthday

....

3 

The day India gained independence

....

4 

The day India became a republic

....

5 

A day to honour our teachers

....

15 August   2 October   26 January

5 September   14 November

Whiz Quiz

Write the names of five special days of India in the correct order.

....

....

19 Food from Plants

We eat roots, stems, leaves, flowers, fruits and seeds of a plant.

Look at the pictures and complete the names of these vegetables.

1. ........AR........O........ is a root. It is long and pointy. It has thin fibres sticking out of its sides. It grows under the ground.

2. ........O........A........O is a stem. It grows under the ground. It is light brown in colour. It has black spots called 'eyes'.

3. ....AB........ ....G........ is a leaf. It is round and firm. It can have many colours like green, white or purple.

4. ........R........CC........ .... is a flower. It is green and looks like a tree with a thick trunk.

5. ....E........ .... are seeds that grow above the ground. Many can be found in a pod. Each one is round and plump and green.

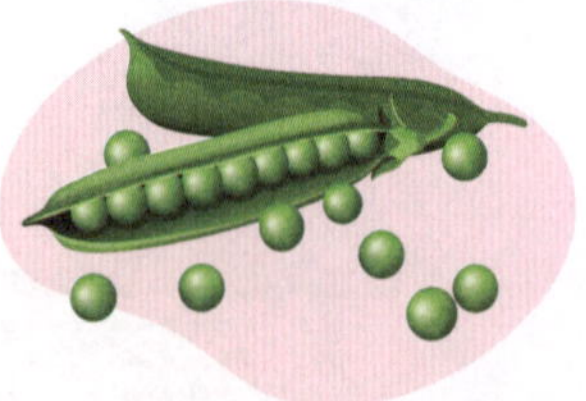

A muskmelon is a large and round yellow-orange fruit. It is grows along the ground. A muskmelon plant has curly stems.

20 Lucky Seven

Complete these lists all of which have seven words. The first letter of each word has been given.

1 **Days of the Week**

S .... T ....
M .... F ....
T .... S ....
W ....

2 **Colours of the Rainbow**

V .... Y ....
I .... O ....
B .... R ....
G ....

3 **Disney's Seven Dwarfs**

D .... S ....
G .... B ....
H .... S ....
D ....

4 **Musical Notes**

D .... S ....
R .... L ....
M .... T ....
F ....

Whiz Fact

There are many more sevens. Sindbad the Sailor made seven voyages and James Bond was Agent 007.

21 Ways We Travel

Look at these vehicles and write their names using the words given in the help box. Write L for vehicles that move on land, W for vehicles that move on water and A for vehicles that move in the air.

1 

....

2 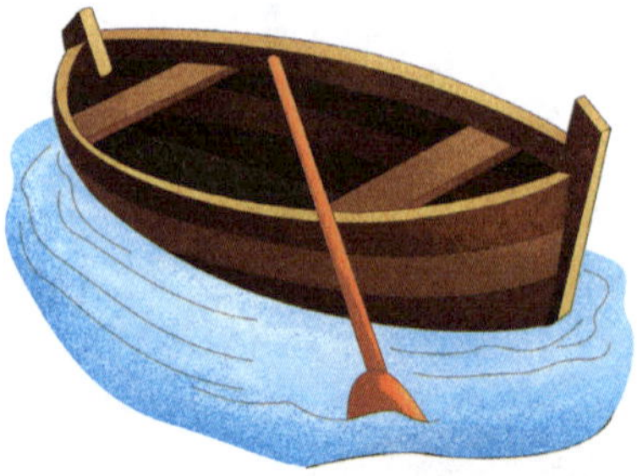

....

3 

....

4 

....

5 

....

6 

....

Whiz Fact

A seaplane is an aircraft that can take off or land on both land and water.

7

....

8

....

9

....

10

....

11

....

12

....

ship bicycle aeroplane autorickshaw train bike
bus boat scooter yacht raft helicopter

Whiz Quiz

Which vehicle can move under the water?

22 Small Creatures

Read the lines about some common insects and complete their names.

1 

I have bright and colourful wings,
From flower to flower I swing!

B........T........E........F........Y

2 I am invisible, though I have mass,
I am as greeny-green as the grass.

GR........SS........O........ ....ER

3 I buzz around blooms and sip precious juice,
I make yummy honey for you!

H........N........ ....B........ ....

4 I march and march like a soldier,
Amongst insects I am a hardworker.

A........ ....

Whiz Quiz

Name two insects you see in your garden.

1 ....

2 ....

5 I live in stagnant water and breed
It is on your blood that I feed!

M........SQ........ ....T........

6 My friends and I love jam and bread
Because of us greeny-grey pests, diseases spread.

HO........S........F........ ....

7 Red and black spots, I am neat as a pin
Grass and leaves, you will find me hiding in.

L........D........BI........ ....

8 I am a big insect, shiny and bright
I whizz in the garden when it is close to night.

DR........G........NF........ ....

9 Do not mess with me, I am a mean thing
If you come too close, you will get a sting!

W........S........

Whiz Fact

Mosquitoes can be dangerous insects. They bite people and spread diseases.

23 Play Safe

Draw a smiling face 🙂 for actions that are safe to do in a park and a sad face ☹ for actions that are unsafe.

1

2

3

4

5

6

7

8

9

Whiz Fact

If you get scratched while playing on a swing, slide or a monkey bar, you must get an injection or you might fall sick.

24 Favourite Characters

Read the lines and write the names of some famous cartoons.

1 

A little white dog whose friend is Charlie Brown.

....

2 

An orange cat whose owner is Jon.

....

3 

A little girl with bright eyes. She has adventures with her friend Boots.

....

4 

A sailor with big arms. He gets strength by eating spinach.

....

5 

A tall and funny dog, he is Mickey's best friend.

....

6 

The queen who can magically create snow.

....

Whiz Fact

Walt Disney created the character Mickey Mouse. He selected many animals such as dogs, cats, frogs and horses and finally chose a mouse and named it Mickey!

25 Uniforms at Work

Many people go to work in a uniform. Look at the pictures of some working people in uniforms. Read the clues and find their names hidden in the grid. One has been done for you.

1

Wears a uniform with bright, glowing stripes. Traffic police

2

Wears a khaki uniform with shiny badges and stars.

....

3

Wears a white uniform and a white cap. ....

4

Wears a space suit and a helmet.

....

5

Wears a uniform with shoulder stripes and a cap.

....

6

Wears a white coat, gloves and a mask.

....

7

Wears a black flowing robe or a black pantsuit.

....

8

Wears a tall hat and an apron.

....

T	R	A	F	F	I	C	P	O	L	I	C	E	D	T	N
L	I	S	O	T	R	S	I	X	P	C	H	O	I	O	U
Z	O	T	B	C	Q	M	L	A	W	Y	E	R	K	D	R
O	W	R	A	L	I	C	O	P	T	Z	F	J	L	U	S
C	G	O	S	D	O	C	T	O	R	I	A	H	A	K	E
H	A	N	N	A	U	N	U	S	R	X	K	J	Z	J	N
E	S	A	M	M	Y	O	F	X	I	C	E	R	W	N	B
T	T	U	I	E	O	U	D	O	C	R	S	E	E	C	M
R	O	T	P	O	L	I	C	E	O	F	F	I	C	E	R

Whiz Fact

Some jobs do not need uniforms, only some special things. A ballet dancer wears pointe shoes and a magician wears a hat.

26 The Ant and the Grasshopper

Long ago, a Greek named Aesop collected many animal stories for children. They are called the Aesop's fables. Here is one of them.

Match the pictures with the correct lines by writing the letters in the boxes.

a The Grasshopper sang all through summer and found herself without food.

b When winter arrived
Not one little bit of fly or worm.

c She set off to cry on the shoulder of her neighbour, the Ant and asked her to lend her a grain or two until the new season. "I will pay you before August, I swear", said the Grasshopper.

d The Ant is no lender
It is her little fault.
"And what exactly were you doing when it was warm?"
She asked the little borrower.

e Oh, day and night
I was singing, singing, did you not hear me?

f So, you were singing? Good for you!
Well, now you can dance.

Whiz Fact

A fable is a story in which animals, birds, insects or even magical creatures are used to tell the story in place of people.

27 Sports Places

Every sport is played in a special space. Match these sports to their special spaces.

1 

a 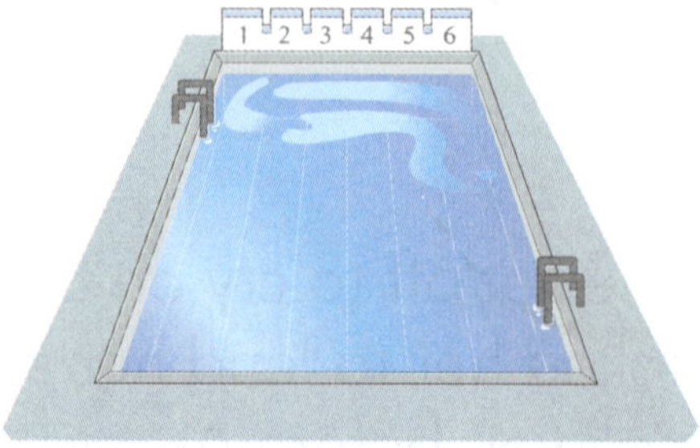

Pool

2 

b 

Court

3 

c 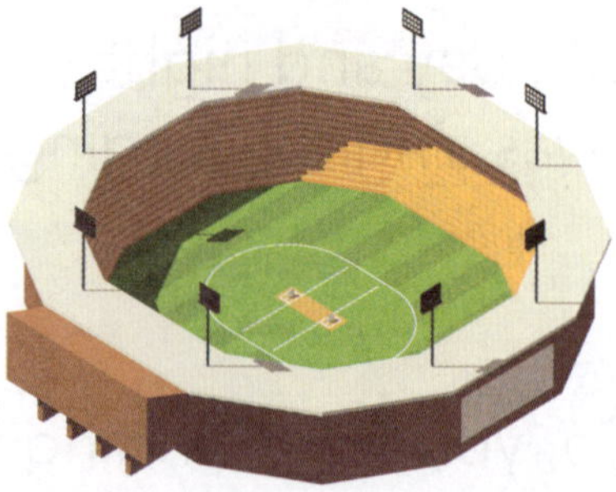

Field

4 

d 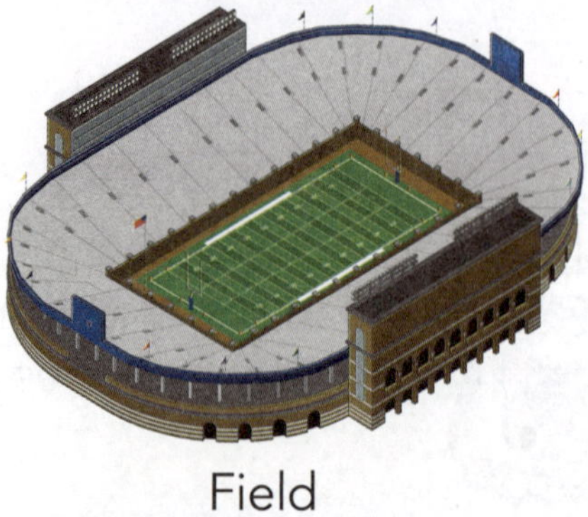

Field

5

e

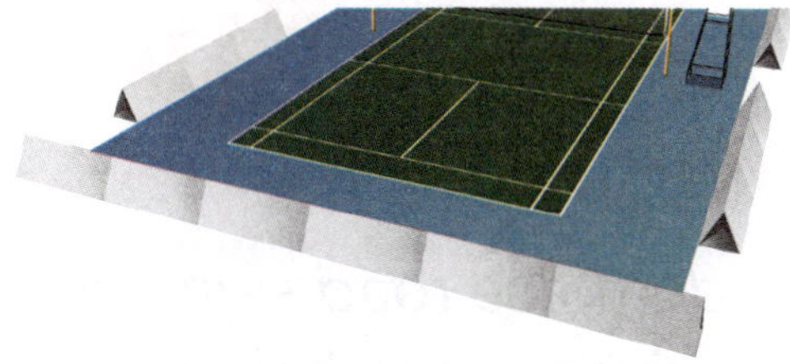

Court

6

f

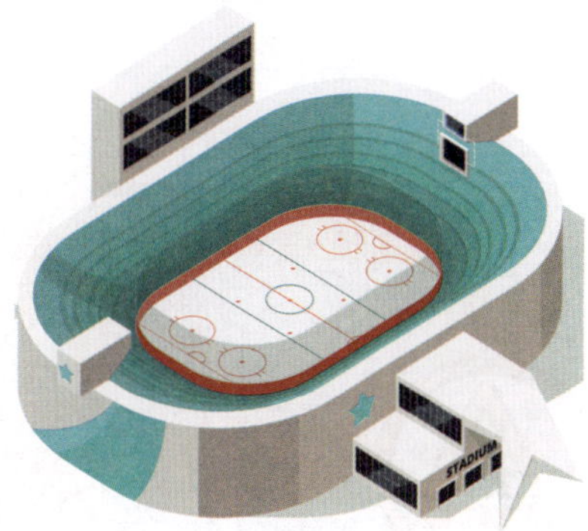

Rink

7

g

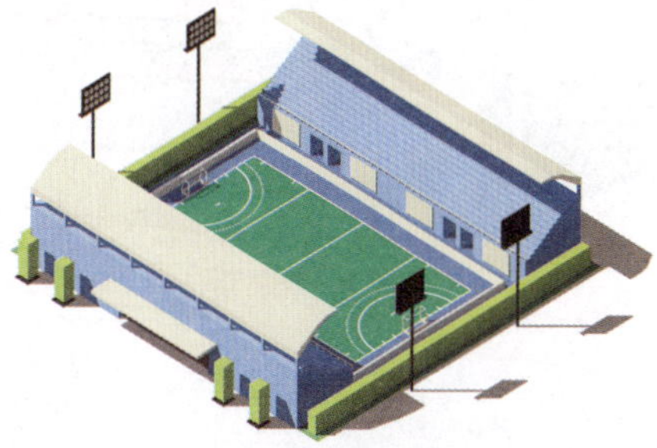

Field

8

h

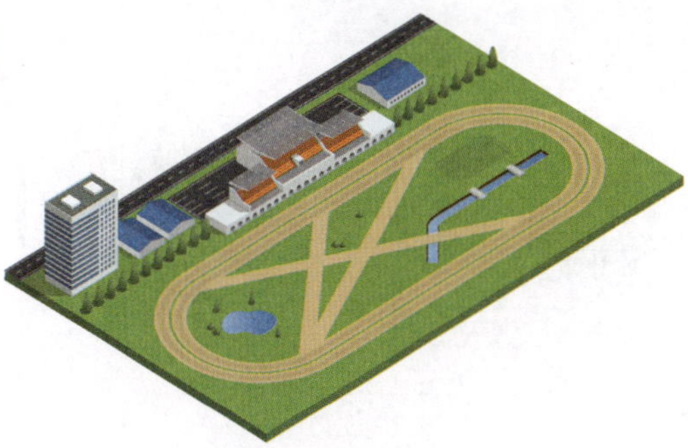

Racecourse

Whiz Fact

Tennis can be played on clay, real grass or artificial grass.

28 On the Road

What do these road signs mean? Write the correct answers using the words given in the help box.

Parking Zebra crossing School Ahead
One-way U-turn Hospital

Learning Skills

CRITICAL THINKING

29 In the Park

Solve the riddles and write the names of things found in a children's park. One has been done for you.

1 My first three letters are same as those of Monday. Mon

My last three letters open a lock. key

My second word rhymes with jar. Bar

Monkey Bar

2 My first letter is the nineteenth letter of the alphabet. ....

My last four letters are a bird's arm.

....

....

3 My first word means a thick forest. ....

My second word rhymes with the word him. ....

....

4 I am just one word.

You climb me and then whoosh down.

....

5 My first word means happy. ....

My second word is go. ....

My third word is the shape of a circle.

....

....

6 My first word is what we do with our eyes. ....

My second word is an object used for cutting wood. ....

....

7 My first word is what a desert is made of ....

My second word rhymes with the word sit. ....

....

8 My first four letters are those of a small train in a city. ....

My next two letters are go.

My last four letters are a long and thin mark. ....

....

Many parks have a narrow entrance with a turning door called turnstile.

30 Beautiful Blooms

Read the lines about some flowers and complete their names.

1

L........T........S is the national flower of India. It grows in ponds. It has floating leaves.

2

M........ ........I........O........D is a golden yellow or orange flower. It is used for making garlands.

3

J........S........I........E is a small white flower. It has a lovely scent. It is used to make flower-strings and perfumes.

4

R........ ....E has a lovely scent and soft petals. It has many colours like red, pink, yellow, white, and its stems have sharp thorns.

5

D........ ....L........A is a large brightly-coloured flower with long stems.

Whiz Quiz

Name two flowers we eat.

1 ....

2 ....

31 Animal and Bird Logos

Many companies use animals or birds in their logos.

Match these companies to their logos with the help of the clues.

	Company		Clue
1	Nestlé	a	A big animal with lots of sharp teeth
2	Twitter	b	A roaring animal with a mane
3	Lacoste	c	A bird which does not sleep at night
4	Trip Advisor	d	Mommy bird with baby bird
5	Metro Goldwyn Mayer	e	An Australian animal whose baby is in its pocket
6	Qantas	f	Little bird

Whiz Fact

An aeroplane is like a big flying bird. Many national airlines like Japan Airlines and Singapore Airlines have birds as their logos.

32 India Tourism

Read the lines about some of the famous buildings and monuments of India and write their names using the words given in the help box.

1 The .... has four pointy towers at four corners. It is in Hyderabad.

2 The .... is a tall red and white tower. It is in New Delhi.

3 The .... is next to the sea. It is in Mumbai.

4 The .... is covered in gold foil. It is in Amritsar.

5 The .... is made of pure white marble. It has four towers at four corners and gardens around. It is in Agra.

6 The .... has a large white dome. It is named after a Queen of England. It is in Kolkata.

7 The .... is red and white. The wind can pass through its many windows. It is in Jaipur.

8 The .... is a temple that looks like a huge chariot on wheels, pulled by horses.

Gateway of India   Charminar   Hawa Mahal   Qutub Minar
Golden Temple   Taj Mahal   Victoria Memorial
Konark Sun Temple

Whiz Fact

The India Gate in New Delhi is a memorial to the soldiers who fought bravely and lost their lives for the country.

33 Water on the Earth

Water is found in many places on the Earth. Read the lines and write the name of the form of water using the words given in the help box.

1

Bigger than any sea

....

2

A white blanket of light flakes

....

3

A body of water flowing into the sea

....

4

A small body of water where fish and frogs live

....

5

Many streams of water falling off a cliff

....

6

Drops of water on leaves, flowers and grass

....

7

Small rocks of ice falling from the sky

....

8

A large area of fresh water, surrounded by land

....

pond hail snow lake waterfall river dew ocean

Whiz Fact

A large part of the Earth is covered with water. Therefore, the Earth is called the 'blue planet'.

34 First Aid Kit

When a person gets hurt or falls ill suddenly, first aid is given before visiting or calling a doctor. First aid kits are kept in schools, offices and malls.

Find the names of 10 things that are kept in a first aid kit from the word grid.

G	L	O	V	E	S	T	T	T	O	R	X	M	O	T
L	Q	P	H	J	C	M	O	R	P	T	R	C	V	H
O	N	J	L	A	I	E	R	T	C	H	K	R	B	E
W	P	J	M	S	S	D	C	O	O	E	M	E	R	R
E	T	H	N	T	O	I	H	R	T	R	E	A	Y	M
R	G	L	O	X	R	C	B	H	T	L	D	M	K	O
B	A	N	D	A	I	D	S	P	O	M	I	O	P	M
F	A	N	T	I	P	R	S	Q	N	O	C	E	O	E
S	C	I	S	S	O	R	S	W	W	T	I	G	T	T
X	P	L	A	S	S	I	R	H	O	L	N	L	R	E
B	A	D	A	G	E	O	H	X	O	A	E	A	A	R
V	O	Y	T	V	E	T	N	Q	L	N	S	S	N	O
B	A	N	D	A	G	E	O	F	E	T	U	T	T	A
R	I	V	R	X	Z	M	L	D	F	I	O	R	R	C
E	V	B	X	A	N	T	I	S	E	P	T	I	C	B

1

Cream

2
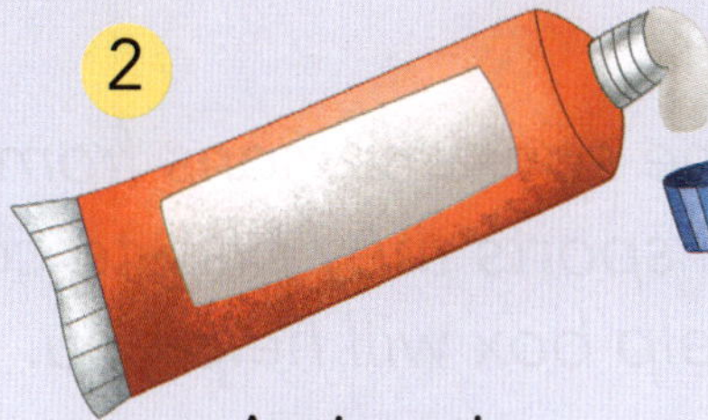
Antiseptic

3
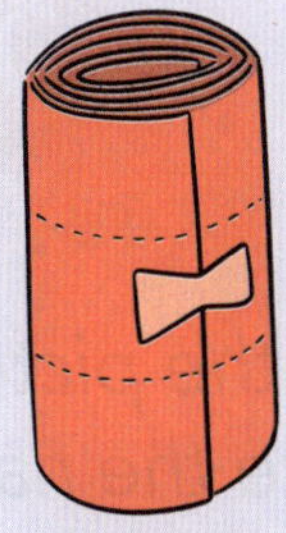
Bandage

4
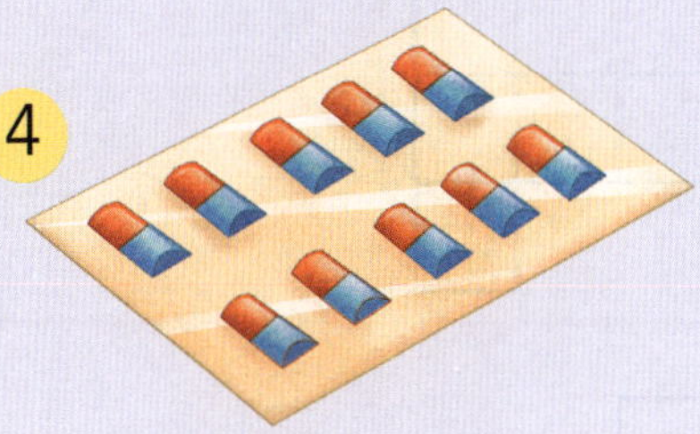
Medicines

5
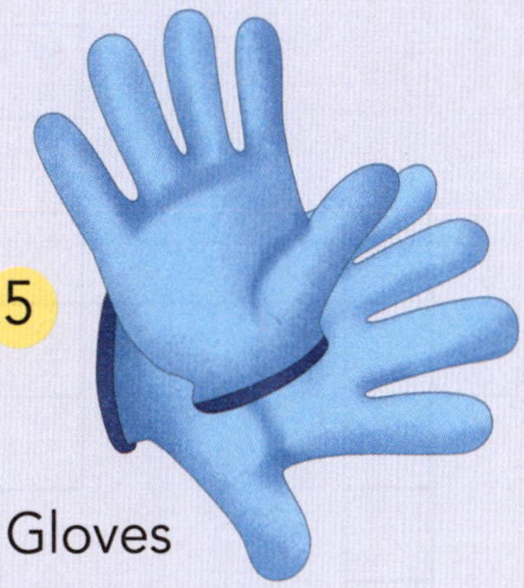
Gloves

6

Cotton wool

7
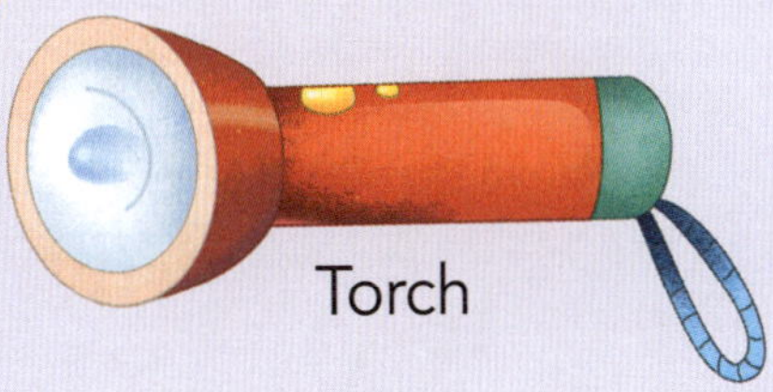
Torch

8
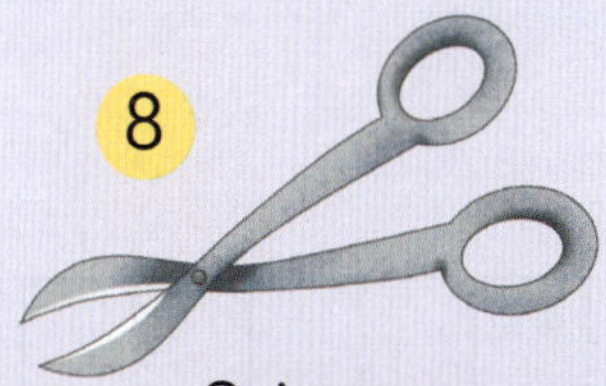
Scissors

9
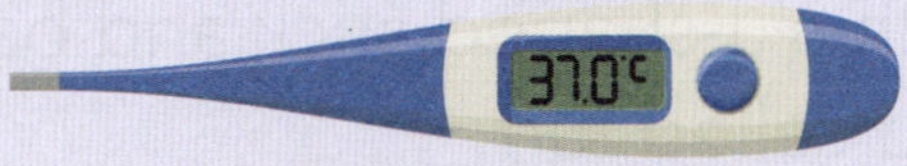

Thermometer

10
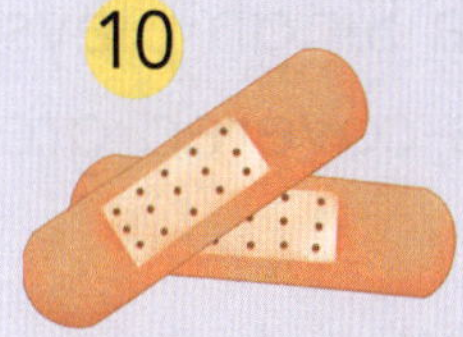
Band Aids

Whiz Fact

First aid kits are usually green or red with a white plus sign on them. These bright colours make it easier to find them during emergencies.

35 Indian Sportspersons

Look at the pictures of some sportspersons from India. Read the clues and write the names of the sports they play to complete the crossword puzzle. The words in the help box will help you.

Across

2 Sardara Singh plays with a J-shaped stick and ball. He plays on a grass-covered ground called turf.

5 Sania Mirza has won many international tournaments. She wears a t-shirt, a wristband and plays with a racquet and a ball.

7 Sakshi Malik wears a shirt called singlet, shorts and light shoes.

8 Saina Nehwal wears a skirt and a shirt. She plays with a racquet and a shuttlecock.

Down

1 Sunil Chhetri is a striker. He wears special shoes called studs, knee socks and a jersey shirt.

3 Vishwanathan Anand is India's first grandmaster. He was once a World Champion. He plays a board game.

4 P.T. Usha was an athlete. She was known as the queen of Indian track and field because she ran very fast.

6 Virat Kohli is a batsman. He wears a helmet, batting pads and gloves. He plays with a bat.

Sardara Singh

Sania Mirza

Saina Nehwal

Sunil Chhetri

Vishwanathan Anand

P.T. Usha

Virat Kohli

Sakshi Malik

Tennis	Running	Badminton	Cricket
Chess	Football	Hockey	Wrestling

Whiz Fact

India's first Olympic champion was Norman Pritchard, a British athlete born in Kolkata. He won two silver medals at the 1900 Olympics.

36 Computer World

Computers are used in homes, schools and offices.

Write the names of parts of a computer or the type of computer. All you need to do is write the names of the things in each picture and then add or subtract letters to form new words.

1 A device used to move a cursor

 – H + M

= ....

2 A small screen bigger than a phone and smaller than a computer

 – LE +  – TER

= ....

3 A part of the computer used for typing

 + 

= ....

4 An object used to charge a laptop or keep a computer plugged in

 + C +  – T

= ....

5 A type of computer we can carry around

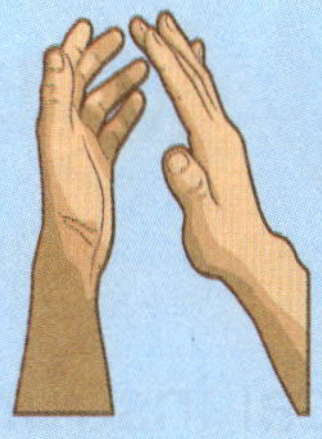 – C + 

= ....

6 A type of computer kept on a table

 + 

= ....

7 A part of the computer found inside it

 + 

= ....

8 A part of the computer on which we see pictures or text

 – EY + I +  – CH

= ....

Whiz Fact

New devices are made constantly in the world of technology and so are new names. A phablet, which is a combination of a tablet and a phone is one such device.

37 Musical Instruments

Look at these musical instruments. Some of them have strings which produce sound when plucked. Some have holes which produce sound when air is blown into them. Some have parts that produce sound when we beat them with hands or sticks.

Write pluck, blow or beat for each of these instruments.

1 I .... the sitar.

2 I .... the trumpet.

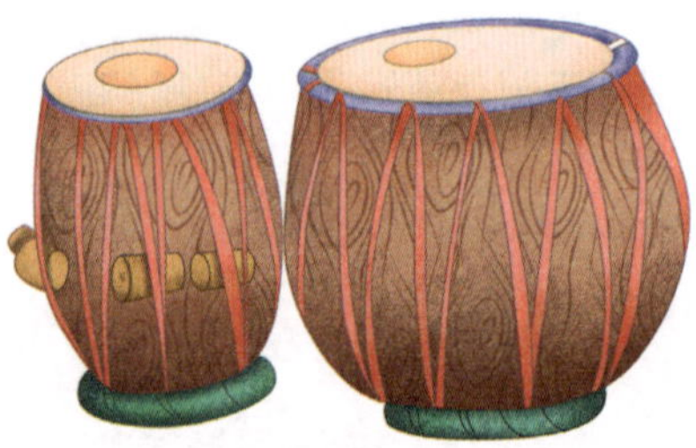

3 I .... the tabla.

4 I .... the saxophone.

5 I .... the drum.

6 I .... the veena.

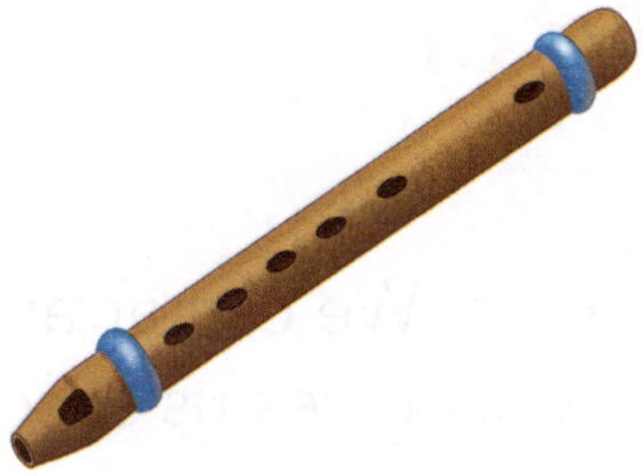

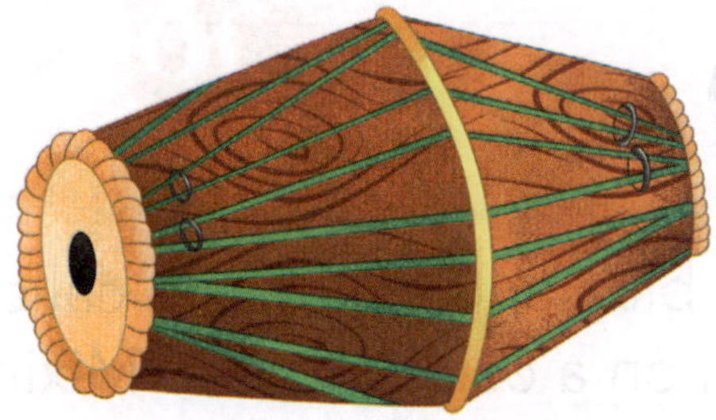

7 I .... the flute.

8 I .... the mridangam.

9 I .... the guitar.

10 I .... the shehnai.

11 I .... the kanjira.

12 I .... the sarod.

Whiz Fact

The first ever musical instruments made by humans were the ones that produce sound when struck or hit. They are called percussion instruments.

38 Colour Wheel

Red, blue and yellow are called the primary colours. We can arrange them on a colour wheel. Mixing two primary colours gives us secondary colours.

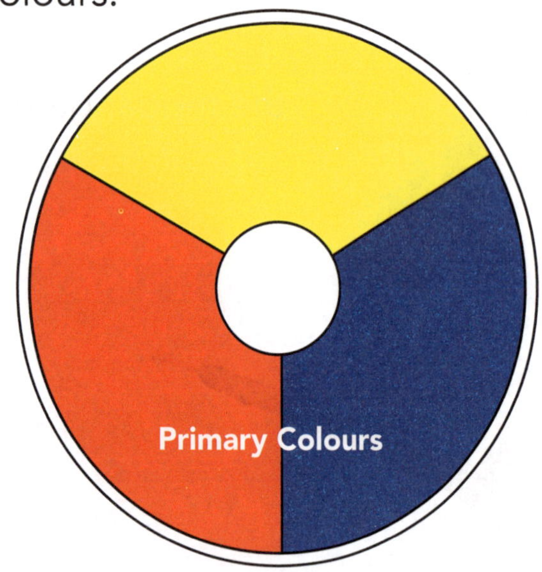

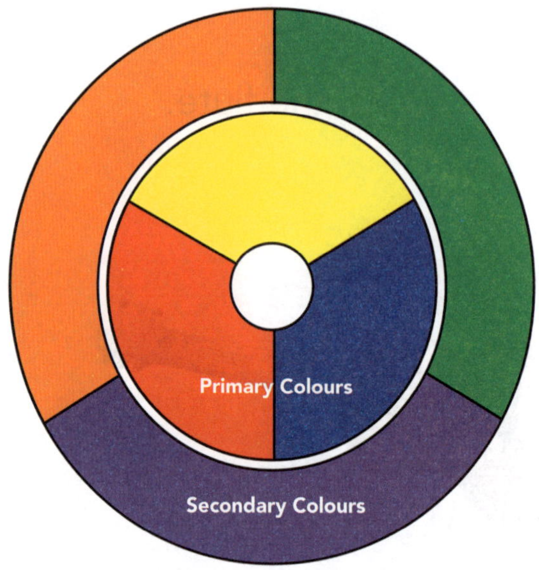

Add the colours in each part of the colour wheel and write the name of the new colour. Then colour the wheel.

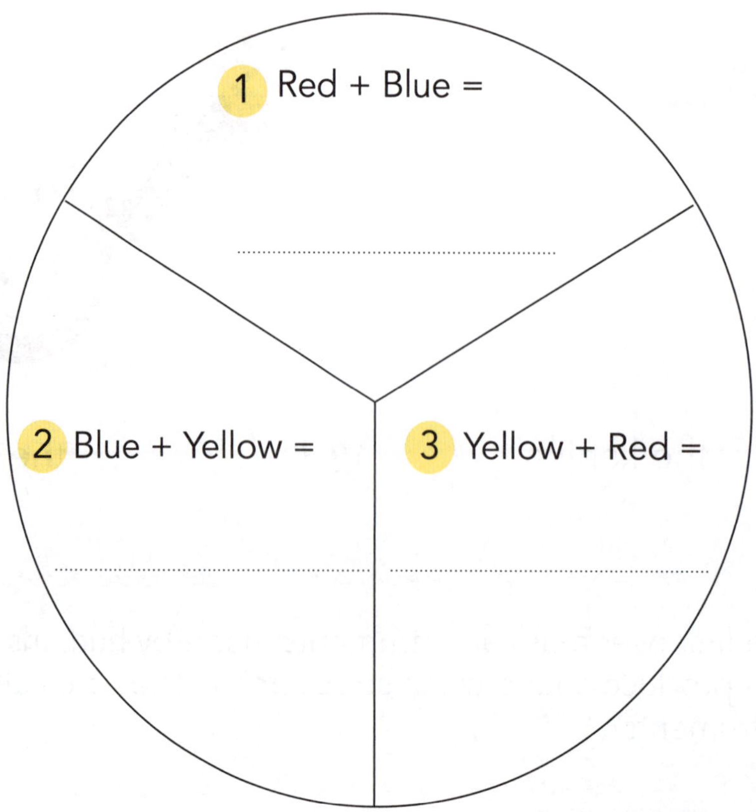

39 Filling Up

Look at these containers. What would you fill them with? Draw a line to join the container to the correct answers.

1 Glass

2 Can

3 Cup

4 Spoon

5 Bucket

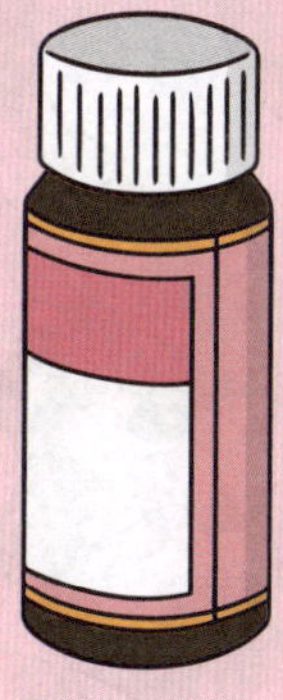

a Syrup

b Milk

c Water

d Tea

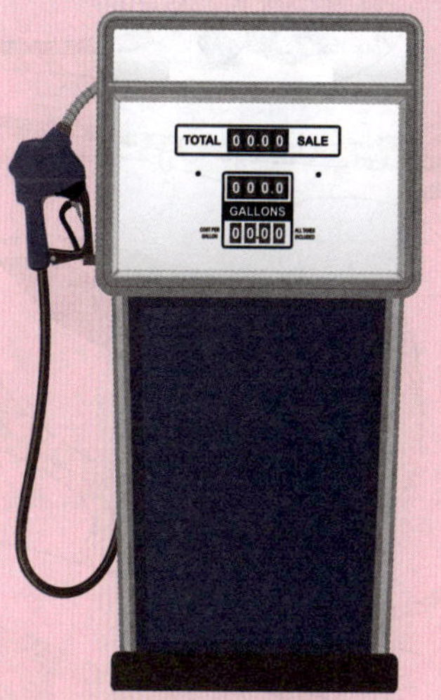

e Petrol

Whiz Fact

Water, syrup or milk take the shape of the container they are poured into.

40 Find the Way

Draw lines on the paths to find out which little bear can reach the goal.

41 Monster Shadows

Tick (✓) the correct pictures to match the shadows to the monsters.

1 

a 

b 

2 

a 

b 

3 

a 

b 

4 

a 

b 

42 Spot the Differences

Find 12 differences between the two pictures.

Quiz Yourself 1

Fill in the blanks with one or two words. Each answer begins with a different letter of the alphabet. Use the words given in the help box.

1. Aesop wrote many animal stories, like *The .... and the Grasshopper.*
2. Red and yellow are two primary colours, the third one is ....
3. A person who makes or repairs shoes is called a ....
4. Another word for wasting time is ....
5. An .... is a huge grey animal with a trunk and tusks.
6. Cricket, football and hockey are played in a ....
7. .... is an old Indian sport played using sticks and stones.
8. A .... flies in the air and has a big fan on top.
9. We can eat an .... in a cone.
10. A lemon is squeezed to make ....
11. The Sun Temple in .... looks like a huge chariot pulled by elephants.
12. .... is India's national flower.

field	ant	helicopter	blue	Konark	dilly-dally
lotus	ice cream	gilli danda	cobbler	elephant	juice

Quiz Yourself 2

Fill in the blanks with one or two words. Each answer begins with a different letter of the alphabet. Use the words given in the help box.

1 A .... is a device used to move a cursor on screen.

2 A .... wears white uniform and white cap.

3 .... is the shape of an egg.

4 We .... the veena to produce sound.

5 .... is a tall tower and famous monument in Delhi.

6 In India, ... is celebrated on 26 January.

7 .... is a white blanket of light flakes.

8 A person who sews clothes is called a ....

9 A police officer wears a khaki .... with shiny badges and stars.

10 .... is India's first grandmaster.

11 A .... is an insect that can give us a nasty sting.

12 I .... the drum.

beat	pluck	oval	tailor	snow	mouse
uniform	Qutub Minar	wasp	nurse	Republic Day	
Vishwanathan Anand					

Answer Key

Page 9: 2. owl 3. crow 4. swan 5. parrot 6. peacock

Page 10-11: 1. see; 2. hear; 3. see; 4. taste; 5. hear; 6. taste; 7. smell; 8. feel; 9. smell

Page 12-13: 1. excuse me; 2. congratulations; 3. yay; 4. hello; 5. thank you; 6. I am sorry; 7. goodnight; 8. please

Page 14-15: 1. i; 2. e; 3. f; 4. d; 5. b; 6. c; 7. g; 8. h; 9. a; 10. j

Page 16-17: 2. dong; 3. knack; 4. top; 5. patter; 6. tock; 7. dally; 8. pong; 9. dumpty; 10. zag

Page 18-19: 1. circle; 2. rectangle; 3. triangle; 4. square; 5. rectangle; 6. oval; 7. triangle; 8. rectangle; 9. oval; 10. circle; 11. square; 12. oval; 13. circle; 14. triangle

Page 20: 1.e; 2. c; 3. d; 4. a; 5. b

Page 21: 1. ×; 2. ✓; 3. ×; 4. ×; 5. ✓; 6. ×

Page 22-23: 1. gardener; 2. carpenter; 3. painter; 4. tailor; 5. potter; 6. cobbler; 7. jeweller; 8. baker

Page 24-25: Across: 2. camel; 4. shark; 6. seal; 7. polar bear; 8. kangaroo; 10. gorilla

Down: 1. rhinoceros; 3. elephant; 5. hippopotamus 9. giraffe

Page 26-27: a. 3, 6, 11, 13; b. 2, 10, 14, 16; c. 1, 7, 9, 12; d. 4, 5, 8, 15

Page 28-29: 1. e; 2. c; 3. d; 4. a; 5. b; 6. j; 7. i; 8. g; 9. h; 10. f

Page 30-31: 2. 3, 1, 2; 3. 2, 3, 1; 4. 2, 3, 1; 5. 1, 3, 2; 6. 3, 1, 2; 7. 2, 3, 1; 8. 3, 2, 1

Page 32-33: 1. kite flying; 2. gilli danda; 3. skipping; 4. marbles; 5. seven stones; 6. hide-and-seek; 7. kho kho; 8. hopscotch

Page 34-35: 1. lamp; 2. bow; 3. O; 4. door; 5. floor; 6. playthings; 7. face; 8. star; 9. baby

Page 36-37: 1. stable; 2. kennel; 3. shed; 4. pond; 5. coop; 6. pen

Page 38: 1. cricket; 2. chess; 3. football; 4. basketball

Page 39: 1. 2 October; 2. 14 November; 3. 15 August; 4. 26 January; 5. 5 September

Page 40: 1. carrot; 2. potato; 3. cabbage; 4. broccoli; 5. peas

Page 41: 1. Sunday, Monday, Tuesday, Wednesday, Thursday, Friday, Saturday; 2. violet, indigo, blue, green, yellow, orange, red; 3. Doc, Grumpy, Happy, Dopey, Sleepy, Bashful, Sneezy; 4. Do, Re, Me, Fa, Sol, La, Ti

Page 42-43: 1. aeroplane, A; 2. boat, W; 3. bus, L; 4. train, L; 5. cycle, L; 6. raft, W; 7. bike, L; 8. helicopter, A; 9. scooter, L; 10. yacht, W; 11. autorickshaw, L; 12. ship, W

Page 44-45: 1. butterfly; 2. grasshopper; 3. honeybee; 4. ant; 5. mosquito; 6. housefly; 7. ladybird; 8. dragonfly; 9. wasp

Page 46: 1. ☹; 2. ☺; 3. ☹; 4. ☺; 5. ☹; 6. ☹; 7. ☺; 8. ☹; 9. ☹

Page 47: 1. Snoopy; 2. Garfield; 3. Dora the Explorer; 4. Popeye; 5. Goofy; 6. Elsa

Page 48-49: 2. police officer; 3. nurse; 4. astronaut; 5. pilot; 6. doctor; 7. lawyer; 8. chef

T	R	A	F	F	I	C	P	O	L	I	C	E	D	T	N
L	I	S	O	T	R	S	I	X	P	C	H	O	I	O	U
Z	O	T	B	C	Q	M	L	A	W	Y	E	R	K	D	R
O	W	R	A	L	I	C	O	P	T	Z	F	J	L	U	S
C	G	O	S	D	O	C	T	O	R	I	A	H	A	K	E
H	A	N	N	A	U	N	U	S	R	X	K	J	Z	J	N
E	S	A	M	M	Y	O	F	X	I	C	E	R	W	N	B
T	T	U	I	E	O	U	D	O	C	R	S	E	E	C	M
R	O	T	P	O	L	I	C	E	O	F	F	I	C	E	R

Page 50-51: 1. a; 2. f; 3. c; 4. d; 5. e; 6. b

Page 52-53: 1. c; 2. d; 3. b; 4. a; 5. g; 6. h; 7. f; 8. e

Page 54-55: 1. School ahead; 2. U-turn; 3. Parking; 4. Hospital; 5. Zebra crossing; 6. One-way

Page 56-57: 2. swing; 3. jungle gym; 4. slide; 5. merry-go-round; 6. seesaw; 7. sandpit; 8. trampoline

Page 58: 1. lotus; 2. marigold; 3. jasmine; 4. rose; 5. dahlia

Page 59: 1. d; 2. f; 3. a; 4. c; 5. b; 6. e

Page 60-61: 1. Charminar; 2. Qutub Minar; 3. Gateway of India; 4. Golden Temple; 5. Taj Mahal; 6. Victoria Memorial; 7. Hawa Mahal; 8. Konark Sun Temple

Page 62-63: 1. ocean; 2. snow; 3. river; 4. pond; 5. waterfall; 6. dew; 7. hail; 8. lake

Page 64-65:

G	L	O	V	E	S	T	T	T	O	R	X	M	O	T
L	Q	P	H	J	C	M	O	R	P	T	R	C	V	H
O	N	J	L	A	I	E	R	T	C	H	K	R	B	E
W	P	J	M	S	S	D	C	O	O	E	M	E	R	R
E	T	H	N	T	O	I	H	R	T	R	E	A	Y	M
R	G	L	O	X	R	C	B	H	T	L	D	M	K	O
B	A	N	D	A	I	D	S	P	O	M	I	O	P	M
F	A	N	T	I	P	R	S	Q	N	O	C	E	O	E
S	C	I	S	S	O	R	S	W	W	T	I	G	T	T
X	P	L	A	S	S	I	R	H	O	L	N	L	R	E
B	A	D	A	G	E	O	H	X	O	A	E	A	A	R
V	O	Y	T	V	E	T	N	Q	L	N	S	S	N	O
B	A	N	D	A	G	E	O	F	E	T	U	T	T	A
R	I	V	R	X	Z	M	L	D	F	I	O	R	R	C
E	V	B	X	A	N	T	I	S	E	P	T	I	C	B

Page 66-67: Across: 2. hockey; 5. tennis; 7. wrestling; 8. badminton

Down: 1. football; 3. chess; 4. running; 6. cricket

Page 68-69: 1. mouse; 2. tablet; 3. keyboard; 4. power cable; 5. laptop; 6. desktop; 7. motherboard; 8. monitor

Page 70-71: 1. pluck; 2. blow; 3. beat; 4. blow; 5. beat; 6. pluck; 7. blow; 8. beat; 9. pluck; 10. blow; 12. beat; 13. pluck

Page 72: 1. purple; 2. green; 3. orange

Page 73: 1. b; 2. e; 3. d; 4. a; 5. c

Page 74: Bear A will reach the goal

Page 75: 1. a; 2. b; 3. b; 4. a

Page 76:

Page 77: 1. Ant; 2. blue; 3. cobbler; 4. dilly-dally; 5. elephant; 6. field; 7. gilli danda; 8. helicopter; 9. ice cream; 10. juice; 11. Konark; 12. lotus

Page 78: 1. mouse; 2. nurse; 3. oval; 4. pluck; 5. Qutub Minar; 6. Republic Day; 7. snow; 8. tailor; 9. uniform; 10. Vishwanathan Anand; 11. wasp; 12. beat